I have collected these special recipes as examples of the best dishes available from one of the most famous cities in the world, Charleston, South Carolina. Many thanks to the innovative chefs and restauranteurs who so graciously shared these delicious and easy to recreate recipes.

I love Charleston. I love this cookbook, and so will you!

A Taste of Charleston is dedicated to my husband, Fred, and to my charming and handsome son, Ellio

Eat and Enjoy!

Phyllis

Ambrosia Bread &
32 Windermere Boul
South Wendermere Shopp...
Charleston

CHOCOLATE MOUSSE

¼ lb. dark chocolate
1 cup egg yolks
1 qt. heavy cream, whipped to a soft peak

1 cup heavy cream
4 oz. sugar

Melt one cup heavy cream with dark chocolate over a double boiler. Remove from heat and let cool to room temperature. Whip the quart of heavy cream, then place in refrigerator. Whip egg yolks and sugar until pale and thick, approximately 2-3 minutes. Fold egg mixture into the chocolate, and then fold in the whipped cream.

Ashly Inn
201 Ashley Avenue
Charleston

PEACHES & CREAM STUFFED WAFFLES & PRALINE SAUCE

WAFFLE BATTER
4 cups waffle mix • 1½ cups milk
1½ cups water
3 eggs • 2 tsp. vanilla
2 tsp. orange extract

FILLING
12 oz. cream cheese • 1 tsp. orange extract
½ cup confectioners' sugar
Sprigs of mint, optional
Whip together with electric mixer.

Mix all together. Prepare waffles and spread 1½ tbsps. filling on ½ of waffle. Top with peach slices and fold over. Top with praline sauce and garnish with a dollop of sour cream, more peach slices and a sprig of mint.

PRALINE SAUCE
2 cups brown sugar
1 stick butter
½ cup water (or maple syrup)

1 cup whole pecans
½ cup sour cream

Combine ingredients and melt in a saucepan. Add ½ cup water (or maple syrup) to thin and 1 cup whole pecans.

Atlanticville

2063 Middle Street
Sullivan's Island

FRESH CHIRMOL

2 medium ripe tomatoes, peeled, seeded & finely diced
½ medium sweet onion (Vidalia or Walla Walla), finely diced
2 scallions (white & green parts), finely chopped
2 Charleston hot chilies, seeded & finely chopped (*for a spicy Chirmol, leave the seeds in*)

2 radishes, finely chopped	1 clove garlic, minced
3 tbsp. chopped fresh cilantro	3 tbsp. olive oil
2 tbsp. distilled white vinegar	2 tbsp. cold water
1 tbsp. fresh lime juice, or more to taste	coarse salt (Kosher or Sea) to taste
½ tsp. freshly ground black pepper	

Combine all the ingredients in a serving bowl and stir to mix. Correct the seasoning, adding lime juice or salt. The chirmol should be highly seasoned. Serve within a few hours of making.

A.W. Shucks

70 State Street
Charleston

SHRIMP FRIED RICE

1 pint whole grain rice	1 large onion, chopped
2½ tsp. salt	2 eggs, beaten
¼ cup cooking oil	1½ tsp. soy sauce
1 cup bean sprouts	salt & pepper to taste

1 lb. shrimp, cooked, peeled & deveined

Bring 6½ quarts of water to a boil, add 1 pint of rice and 2½ tsps. salt. Cook rice until tender, stirring occasionally. When rice is cooked, pour into a colander to drain.

Cut shrimp lengthwise and set aside. Heat oil in a heavy skillet. Stir in shrimp and onion. Beat eggs and add to pan, stir and cook 2½ minutes. Stir in rice and continue to cook another 3 minutes. Sprinkle soy sauce over all and mix well. Add the bean sprouts and cook 3 minutes longer. Season with salt & pepper.

Baker's Cafe
214 Kings Street
Charleston

BROCCOLI ALMOND CHICKEN SALAD

2 cups cooked broccoli florets
1 cup slivered toasted almonds
4 tbsp. honey
½ cup mayonnaise

2 cups red seedless grapes (whole)
¼ cup poppy seed
½ cup sour cream

4 cups cooked chicken, chopped chunky

Mix all ingredients in a large bowl. Add more sour cream and mayonnaise if needed.

Bessinger's Bar-B-Que & Buffeteria

1602 Savannah Hwy.
Charleston

SWEET POTATO SOUFFLÉ

6 medium sweet potatoes
3 tbsp. butter
2 eggs, beaten
½ tsp. salt
cinnamon

½ cup light brown sugar
¼ cup raisins
¼ cup sugar
¼ cup coconut

Preheat oven to 350°. Cook, peel and mash the sweet potatoes. Add butter and eggs to potatoes and beat until light and fluffy. Add all the remaining ingredients, reserving a little coconut. Place in a buttered 2 quart casserole, and sprinkle with cinnamon. Bake for about 30 minutes. A few minutes before removing from oven, sprinkle with remaining coconut and brown.

SCALOPPINI OF VEAL WITH MARSALA WINE SAUCE, MUSHROOMS, PROSCIUTTO HAM, DRIED TOMATOES & ANGEL HAIR PASTA

1.5 - 2 lb. Veal Top Round, or pounded Scallopini
Salt & Pepper to Taste

½ cup flour
Olive Oil as needed

Slice veal into 1¾ ounce pieces, cover with plastic and pound with a mallet to tenderize and flatten. Do not pulverize. Reserve.

Ingredients for Sauce:

3 tbsp. olive oil, blend
2 tsp. garlic, minced
½ cup Shiitake mushroom caps, julienned
½ cup Crimini mushrooms, quartered
¼ cup fresh basil, julienned

½ cup shallot, minced
1/3 cup dried tomatoes, julienned
1 cup Marsala wine
2 cups browned veal stock, reduced
salt & pepper to taste

4 oz. Prosciutto ham, sliced 1/16 inch thick, then julienned

Ingredients for Pasta:

8 oz. fresh Angel Hair Pasta   3 tbsp. whole butter   1 tsp. chopped garlic
3 tbsp. assorted chopped herbs, parsley, basil, chives, chervil, oregano

Assemble all the above ingredients. Season the veal with salt & pepper. Dredge in the flour and shake off excess. Sauté in the oil blend 3-4 at a time cooking until just done. Place on a plate until all are cooked. Use an even heat, careful not to burn the caramelized bits that may accumulate on the bottom of the pan. In the same pan, start the sauce by adding a little oil if needed. Sauté the shallots with the garlic until translucent. Add the mushrooms and cook another minute. Add the prosciutto and then deglaze with the Marsala wine and allow reducing by 2/3. Add the veal stock, dried tomatoes, basil and salt and pepper. Reduce by 1/3 over medium high heat. Add the cooked pasta with the melted butter, garlic and herbs. Place a nest of the pasta on top of the plate and shingle three pieces of the veal in front of it. Coat with a nice portion of the sauce and all of its ingredients.

Bocci's Italian Restaurant
158 Church Street
Charleston

BASIL PESTO

3 oz. fresh basil
½ cup pine nuts or walnuts
2 tbsp. chopped garlic
1 tbsp. black pepper

3 oz. fresh spinach
½ cup grated parmesan
½ cup olive oil
1 tbsp. salt

Pour all ingredients into a food processor and blend until smooth.
Yield: 2 cups.

Boone Hall Plantation
Serena's Kitchen
Mt. Pleasant

FRIED GREEN TOMATOES

5 - 8 large green tomatoes	½ cup all purpose flour
1 cup Italian style breadcrumbs	¼ cup yellow cornmeal
1 cup grated parmesan cheese	garlic salt, black pepper & cayenne to taste

EGG WASH

3 eggs	¼ cup milk
dash of salt	1 cup flour

Slice tomatoes fairly thin. Not too thin! Combine bread crumbs, cheese, flour, cornmeal and spices in a bowl big enough to dredge the tomatoes. Make egg wash and put in another bowl. You will need one more bowl for the remaining cup of flour. Dip each tomato slice first in flour, then in egg wash, and finally in the breadcrumb mixture. Fry in vegetable oil at 350°, until golden brown, 2 to 4 minutes, turning occasionally to brown evenly. Drain on paper towels and serve with a sour cream dill sauce.

SOUR CREAM DILL SAUCE

1 cup sour cream	½ cup Dukes mayonnaise
1½ tbsp. dried or fresh dill	juice of ½ lemon

garlic, salt & pepper to taste (may substitute Salad Supreme for the salt & pepper)

Bull & Finch Restaurant & Pub
Mt. Pleasant, Downtown, West Ashley

BEEF WELLINGTON

2 tbsp. neutral oil, grapeseed
4 tbsp. Duxelles, recipe below
1 egg yolk, beaten

2 6-8 oz. beef tenderloin filets
salt & pepper

2 4"x4" puff pastry sheets, slightly cooler than room temperature

Heat sauté pan to medium-high heat. Season filets with salt & pepper liberally on each side. Add oil and brown top and bottom of filets. Remove and place on kitchen towel. Spread 1 tbsp. duxelles in middle of each sheet. Place a filet on each and spread 1 more tbsp. duxelle on top of filet. Bring corners of pastry together, wrapping the filets completely. Invert and shape with your hands until rounded and sealed. Brush top of pastry with egg glaze and bake in a 350° pre-heated oven for 20-25 minutes, rare to medium rare. For a traditional version season & sear a ½ inch slice of foie gras and place on pastry sheets first.

1 tbsp. cooking oil
2 sprigs thyme

1 tbsp. shallots, finely chopped
salt & pepper

2-3 drops sherry vinegar (or any vinegar acid such as lemon juice)
1 cup mushrooms, finely diced (cremini preferred, white domestics work fine)

Heat sauté pan to medium heat. Add oil and shallots and sweat until translucent. Add thyme sprigs and mushrooms. Cook until mushrooms have given up their liquid and then reduce until nearly dry. Remove thyme sprigs and season to taste with salt, pepper & vinegar.

Café Cafe
177 Meeting Street
Charleston

FRENCH TOAST STRADA

1 lb. loaf unsliced French bread, cut into 1" cubes • 8 eggs
1 8oz. pkg. cream cheese, cut into ½" cubes • 6 tbsp. melted butter
2½ cups light cream or half & half • ¼ cup maple syrup

Grease a 3-qt. rectangular baking dish. Place half the bread cubes in the dish. Top with cream cheese cubes and then the remaining bread cubes. Combine eggs, cream, melted butter and syrup. Mix well and pour over bread and cheese cubes. Using a spatula, slightly press layers down to moisten. Cover with plastic wrap and let sit for 2 to 24 hours. Remove plastic wrap and bake uncovered for 35 to 40 minutes or until set and golden brown. Let stand about 10 minutes before cutting. Top with apple cider syrup, a big dollop of whipped cream and a sprig of fresh mint.

APPLE CIDER SYRUP

½ cup sugar	4 tsp. cornstarch
½ tsp. cinnamon	1 cup apple juice
1 tbsp. lemon juice	2 tbsp. butter

Combine sugar, cornstarch and cinnamon in a small saucepan. Stir in apple juice and lemon juice. Cook and stir over medium heat until thickened and bubbly. Cook for two more minutes. Remove from heat and add butter.

Carolina's
10 Exchange Street • Charleston

CAROLINA PEA CAKES

PEA MIX

24 oz. black eyed peas
¾ gallon water
1 oz. chicken base
1 smoked ham hock

3 large onions, diced
3 tsp. garlic, chopped
2 jalapenos or 1 tsp. **"Joe Mike"** Habanero

Bring all the ingredients to a boil. Lower heat and simmer, stirring frequently. When peas are fully cooked, remove ham hock. Drain broth and reserve for later use as soup base.

SEASONING MIX

¼ tsp. salt
¼ tsp. dry mustard
Pinch cumin

1 tbsp. thyme
¼ tsp. black pepper

½ tsp. basil
1 tbsp. oregano

Mix all seasoning ingredients together and add to peas.

HERB & VEGETABLE MIX

2 tbsp. garlic, chopped
2 tbsp. bell pepper, chopped
2 jalapenos, chopped
3 tbsp. parsley

2 green onions, chopped
2 tbsp. red onion, chopped
1 tbsp. yellow onion, chopped
2 tbsp. fresh cilantro

Place all herb & vegetable ingredients in a food processor and mince, but not too fine. Make into small patties. Then sauté in extra virgin olive oil over low heat for 5 minutes and set aside to cool.

BLUE CHEESE BUTTER

¼ lb. blue cheese
1 tsp. sugar
1 tsp. black pepper
2 tbsp. parsley, fresh & chopped
1 garlic clove, chopped fine

¼ lb. butter
1 tsp. salt
1 tbsp. thyme, fresh & chopped
3 tbsp. red onion, chopped fine

Put all ingredients in mixer or food processor. Mix until smooth.
Portion and refrigerate. Serve over pork while hot.

Charleston Crabhouse
Charleston, Mt. Pleasant & James Island

CRAB DIP

1 lb. special (lump) crabmeat

8 oz. machine picked crabmeat (claw)

1 cup shredded cheddar cheese

2 cups shredded mozzarella cheese

1 cup minced celery

5 cups mayonnaise

2 tsp. onion powder

2 tsp. white pepper

In a medium mixing bowl, add all crabmeat and pick for shells. Remove any excess water. Mince two celery stalks and strain. Add to the crabmeat. Add cheeses and seasonings to the crabmeat mixture. Add mayonnaise and mix well. Sprinkle with paprika and refrigerate. Serve cold.

CHARLESTON GRILL BUTTON MUSHROOM SOUP

2½ lbs. button mushrooms, washed
6 shallots, peeled & sliced
6 garlic cloves, chopped
salt & fresh ground white pepper

3 stems fresh thyme
4 oz. butter
½ gallon chicken stock

Heat 1 oz. of the butter in a sauté pan until almost brown. Add ¼ of the mushrooms and let them brown in the pan without shaking them for 30 seconds. Then shake the pan to toss them around a bit. Repeat this until all the mushrooms are browned.

In the last pan of mushrooms, add the shallots and garlic and cook for 2 minutes. Reglaze the pan with ½ cup of the chicken stock. Add this juice from the pan and all the mushrooms to a large pot. Cover with the rest of the stock, thyme, and some salt and pepper. Boil for 15 minutes over a hot flame. Remove the thyme and puree in a blender until smooth. Add salt and pepper to taste. Serve very hot over sautéed wild mushrooms.

CRABCAKE SOUFFLÉ

3 cups crabmeat
2 tbsp. mustard
heavy cream
roasted red pepper purée
2 tbsp. diced red onion
chives

3 Eggs
½ tbsp. Old Bay Seasoning
Mango purée
1 cup diced pineapple
rice wine vinegar

In a food processor add the crabmeat, eggs, mustard and Old Bay seasoning. Purée this mixture. With the processor still running add just enough heavy cream to make the mixture creamy. Reserve crab soufflé mix.

Take the diced pineapple and red onion and mix together in a bowl. Add a splash of vinegar and enough minced chives to add color to this. Thoroughly mix together. Season with salt & pepper.

Preheat the oven to 375°. Fill a 2½ ring mold to the top with the crab soufflé mix. Bake in the oven on wax paper for 12 to 15 minutes or until firm to the touch. Put onto the center of a plate. Garnish the plate with the pineapple relish.

Cisco's Cafe
1114 Sam Rittenburg Blvd.
Charleston

ENCHILADA SAUCE

1 gallon water
1/8 cup salt
4 tbsp. white pepper
1½ cups Wesson oil
1 qt. tomato sauce

3 tbsp. chicken base
1/8 cup garlic salt
2 tsp. margoram leaves
¾ qt. chili pepper powder

ROUX

¾ qt. flour

1 qt. water

Mix water, chicken base, salt, garlic salt, white pepper and margoram leaves. Add oil, chili powder and tomato sauce. Bring to boil. Add roux. Let simmer for 15 minutes.

Coconut Joe's
Isle of Palms

CRABCAKES

1 lb. fresh lump crabmeat
2 green onions, finely chopped
¼ Worchestersire sauce
½ cup Japanese bread crumbs (Kikkoman)
¼ tsp. black pepper
¼ tsp. white pepper

½ cup mayonnaise
½ tsp. Tabasco sauce
½ tbsp. lemon juice
½ tbsp. ground thyme
½ tsp. salt

Combine all ingredients in a large bowl. Form mixture into 3 oz. balls (approx. 8-9 balls). Place on flat wax paper until ready to cook.

Egg Wash: In a small bowl mix 2 eggs and ¼ cup milk. Whip eggs and milk until well mixed.

Flatten crab ball into a cake. Dip in egg wash, then lightly roll in Japanese breadcrumbs. Place crab cakes in a lightly oiled skillet which is preheated. Fry crabcake for 3 minutes on one side and then turn and cook for 1½ minutes.

Cresent Restaurant
626 Coleman Boulevard
Mt. Pleasant

QUAIL WITH SUMMER FRUITS

4 ca. quail (whole or semi-boneless)
2 black plums
1 large white nectarine (or peach)
¼ lb. fresh cherries, pitted & halved
1 cup red wine (pinot noir or zinfandel are best)
¼ cup port wine

Clean the quail and reserve. Cut the nectarine and plums into ¼"
dice. Add the nectarines, plums, cherries, and the wines to a saucepan
and cook over medium-high heat until the fruit softens and the wine
reduces to a semi-thick glaze. Grill or roast the quail to desired
temperature. Serve atop the fruit, spoon the wine glaze around the
plate as the sauce.

Cru Café
18 Pinckney Street, Charleston
GARLIC SEARED SCALLOPS WITH MAINE LOBSTER
PLUM WINE SUCCOTASH & FRIED TARO ROOT

8 U-10 Scallops	2 tbsp. olive oil	4 whole garlic cloves, sliced thin
½ tbsp. cumin	½ Habanero	½ tbsp. chili powder
½ tsp. cayenne	½ tsp. paprika	1 tbsp. olive oil (for cooking)

Salt & Pepper to taste

Take the individual scallop and peel off the small muscle on the side. Discard the muscle. Put all the first nine ingredients in a bowl adding the scallops last. Marinate for at least one hour. Take a 9" sauté pan and heat it up very, very hot. Season scallops with salt and pepper. Add the tablespoon of cooking olive oil and add four scallops to the sauté pan. Sear hard on one side for about 2 minutes. Turn over and cook them on the other side for 2 more minutes. Finish with the butter.

SUCCOTASH

1 tail of Maine lobster	1 red onion
4 cobbs of corn (fresh cut off cobb)	10-15 green beans, small dice
10-15 sugar snap peas, small dice	2 tbsp. olive oil

1 tbsp. garlic • 1 tbsp. shallot • salt & pepper to taste • 1 tbsp. fresh thyme
1 tbsp. basil • 2 oz. plum wine • 4 tbsp. butter (keep at room temp. to soften)
2 oz. lobster stock (optional, but adds great flavor)

Heat a saucepan to very hot. Add olive oil and sauté the shallots and garlic until translucent. Add the lobster meat. Sear the lobster until about two thirds cooked. Add the other cut vegetables and sauté them for a few minutes to sear in the flavors. Deglaze the sauté pan with the wine, and add herbs. Reduce for a couple of minutes until the wine is almost dry in the bottom of the pan. At this point add lobster stock and cook until reduced by half. Finish by slowly adding butter until very creamy. Salt and pepper to taste. Put succotash in center of plate and top with two seared scallops. For the fried taro root slice as thin as you can and cut into very thin strips. Fry in oil until crispy. Finish the plate with the fried taro root.

Cypress
167 E. Bay Street • Charleston

CRISPY BENNE SEED SHRIMP WITH SWEET MUSTARD & HOT CHILI GARLIC SAUCE

1 lb. large white shrimp, peeled & deveined
8-10 whole cilantro leaves, garnish

3 tbsp. salt
3 tbsp. scallions, sliced thin on the bias

Ingredients for batter:

1½ cups all purpose flour
4 tbsp. black sesame seeds (goma seeds)
2 tbsp. chives, sliced fine

1½ cups cornstarch

1 tbsp. parsley, minced

2½ cups soda water, chilled
2 tbsp. white sesame seeds

In a large stainless or glass mixing bowl, mix together cornstarch and flour. Add the soda gradually until forms a smooth thick batter the consistency of pancake batter. Add seeds & herbs. Keep cold and let rest momentarily, reserve.

Ingredients for Mustard Sauce
1 cup honey   1 cup Dijon mustard
          ¼ tsp. sesame oil

Ingredients for Hot Chili Garlic Sauce
2 tsp. hot chili garlic sauce (sambal)
4 tbsp. honey   1 tsp. rice wine vinegar

Wash shrimp and place on paper towel and refrigerate. They must be free of moisture to hold the batter. Mix together ingredients for mustard sauce and reserve. Mix together ingredients for Hot Chili Garlic Sauce and reserve. Preheat frying oil to 360°. Grab shrimp 3 or 4 at a time by the tail and dip into batter. Shake off excess for a second and place in hot oil. While shrimp are frying, lay out plates and drizzle two sauces around using a coffee spoon. Remove shrimp from hot oil and place on absorbent paper. Season with sea salt immediately. Stack shrimp, five each and garnish with scallions & fried cilantro leaves.

Diana's Restaurant
155 Meeting Street
Charleston

CHARLESTON COCONUT CAKE

3½ cups sifted cake flour	4 tsp. baking powder
½ tsp. salt	2 cups sugar
1 cup butter	1 cup milk
1 tsp. vanilla	7 or 8 egg whites
4 cups heavy whipping cream	1 cup powdered sugar
¾ tsp. almond extract	shredded coconut

Preheat oven to 375°. Pre-sift cake flour with baking powder and salt. Cream butter, and add the sifted sugar gradually and continue creaming until very light. Add the flour mixture to the butter mixture in 3 parts, alternately with thirds of 1 cup milk. Stir the batter until smooth after each addition. Beat in vanilla. Whip the egg whites until stiff but not dry. Fold them lightly into the cake batter. Bake in greased pans for about 25 minutes. Cool thoroughly before frosting.

FROSTING

Whip heavy whipping cream, adding powdered sugar and almond extract once the cream begins to thicken. Spread on cooled cake. Cover entire cake with shredded coconut. Refrigerate for two hours or more before cutting.

AWARD WINNING SHE CRAB SOUP

<u>ROUX</u>

¼ lb. butter   ¼ lb. flour

Melt butter and stir in flour to make roux. Add milk and cream. Bring to boil. Add remaining ingredients. Simmer for 20 minutes. Garnish with sherried whipped cream.

<u>SHE CRAB SOUP</u>

1 cup heavy cream	3 cups milk
2 cups fish stock or water & fish base	¼ lb. crab roe
1 lb. white crabmeat	1 cup chopped celery
¼ cup carrots, chopped	¼ cup onion, chopped
¼ cup sherry wine	1 tbsp. Tabasco sauce
1 tbsp. Worcestershire sauce	

Sauté the celery, carrots, onion, with the wine, tabasco sauce and Worcestershire sauce. Combine all above ingredients.

Fantasia
11 George Street
Charleston

FANTASIA'S SPICY PECANS

2 eggs whites, slightly beaten
2 tsps. water
2 (16-oz.) bags shelled pecans
1½ tsps. salt
½ cups sugar

1 tbsp. cinnamon
¼ tsp. nutmeg
¼ tsp. allspice
¼ tsp. ginger

Preheat oven to 300°. Combine egg whites and water. Add nuts and toss to coat. Combine next 6 ingredients. Add to nuts and toss until coated. Place in single layer on lightly greased baking sheet. Bake for 20 to 25 minutes.

Fig Restaurant
232 Meeting Street
Charleston

CHILLED ASPARAGUS SOUP WITH PANCETTA

4 cups fresh chicken stock (substitute vegetable stock or even water)
2 tbsp. good quality olive oil
2 medium sized leeks (white part only), split, washed & sliced crosswise
¼ cup Idaho potatoes, peeled & cut into ½" cubes
1 lb. Asparagus, ½" slice, tough bottoms discarded
2 sprigs fresh thyme (if not available, omit; do not substitute dried)
salt & ground black pepper • Pancetta, sliced thin and julienned
¼ cup crème Fraiche (substitute sour cream or fresh goat cheese)

In a heavy bottomed 4 quart soup pot, add olive oil and pancetta over medium heat until the pancetta becomes crisp. Take the pot off the heat and transfer the pancetta to a plate with a paper towel to drain (for garnish) and leave the remaining oil in the pan. Place the pot back on the stove over medium heat and add the leeks. Cook until the leeks are tender and add the chicken stock, potato and thyme. Bring to a simmer, and when the potato becomes tender, add the asparagus. Cook until the asparagus has no crunch left but is still bright green. Remove from the heat and transfer to a bowl over ice (ice bath). When the soup is cool, remove the thyme and purée in a blender until smooth. Season with salt and pepper and garnish with the pancetta and crème fraiche.

Gilligan's Steamer & Raw Bar
Johns Island & Mt. Pleasant

BAG FISH RECIPE

4-8 oz. portions of fresh Mahi-Mahi   4 cups liquid margarine
2 oz. Old Bay seasoning   2 oz. garlic salt
Fresh vegetables of choice *(we use carrots, broccoli, green bell peppers, squash, onions & snow peas)*

Mix together the margarine, garlic salt and seasoning. Place the uncooked vegetables in the bottom of a brown (lunch sized) paper bag. Place the raw fish on top of the vegetables and pour one cup of the bag fish butter over the vegetables and fish. Cook at 375° for 20-25 minutes. Be careful to drain the bag of excess butter or it will be too salty. Also, it's important to put the vegetables on the bottom or the fish will stick to the bag.

SEARED PEPPERED TUNA WITH ONION CONFIT & A ROASTED BLACK OLIVE CAPER TAPENADE

CONFIT

3-4 oz. portions of yellow fin tuna, in blocks
6-8 oz. extra virgin olive oil
2 oz. rosemary, chopped

10-12 Spanish onions
3-4 cloves chopped garlic
2 oz. thyme, chopped

Peel and slice onion very thin. In a sauté pan, heat extra virgin olive oil to hot and not smoking. Then add onions, garlic & herbs. Slowly cook this for about 2-3 hours.

TAPENADE

6-8 ripe Roma tomatoes
1 oz. capers
1 splash lemon & sherry wine vinegar

1 cup cured black olives
2 oz. extra virgin olive oil

Peel, seed & roughly chop the tomatoes. Place in oven at 220° for 3-4 hours. Season with salt & pepper and a dash of sherry vinegar before they go into the oven. Add extra virgin olive oil when the tomatoes are done. Pit and roughly chop the olives, then add to the cooked tomatoes. Finish with capers, salt, pepper and a dash of lemon.

Hayne House
30 King Street
Charleston

ROBIE'S SAUSAGE & EGG CASSEROLE

1 lb. bulk sausage (mild or spicy)
½ cup chopped mushrooms
1 cup cream or half-and-half
½ cup NY sharp cheddar cheese, grated

3 tbsp. butter
15 eggs

Brown sausage in skillet; crumble and drain. Spread sausage in bottom of a casserole dish. Sauté mushrooms in butter; drain and mix with cream in a separate dish. Soft scramble eggs and layer on top of sausage. Spread mushroom/cream mixture over eggs. Sprinkle grated cheese over top. Cook at 350° for 20 minutes or until cheese is melted and casserole is bubbly.

High Cotton
199 East Bay Street
Charleston

BOURBON GRILLED PORK RIB CHOP

4 8oz. center cut pork rib chops
2 tbsp. chopped fresh thyme
1 cup prepared steak sauce

2 tbsp. canola oil
2 onions, minced
1 cup bourbon

Prepare coals or light gas grill. Heat oil in a small saucepan; add onion, sauté until lightly caramelized. Add thyme, cook one minute longer, and add bourbon. Reduce until most liquid is evaporated. Add steak sauce, set aside to cool.

Grill chops 5 minutes per side, brush with sauce, then move to colder part of grill. Brush with more sauce and serve with additional sauce on the side. Great on ribs, chicken or steak!

Hyman's Seafood

215 Meeting Street
Charleston

COLE SLAW

2 heads green cabbage
½ cup relish
1 tsp. celery seed

½ cup mayonnaise
1/3 cup mustard
½ cup sugar

Shred cabbage, and mix all ingredients together and chill.

J. Bistro
819 Colemans Boulevard
Mt. Pleasant

STEAK RUB

1 tbsp. black pepper	4 tbsp. salt
1 tbsp. cayenne	4 tbsp. paprika
1 tbsp. basil	1 tbsp. white pepper
¼ tsp. nutmeg	2 tbsp. cumin
1 tbsp. oregano	1 tbsp. mustard powder
2 tbsp. garlic powder	1 tbsp. thyme

Combine all ingredients. Season for pork, chicken, beef or fish.

TOMATO CHUTNEY

1 cup onions, julienned   2 cups cider vinegar
2 tbsp. red pepper flakes   2 cups sugar
3 cups Roma tomatoes, julienned with seeds removed

Combine all ingredients.

Kaminsky's
Downtown Charleston

GRAN CRAN POUND CAKE

½ lb. butter
6 large eggs, added one at a time
3 large oranges, zested & juiced
3¼ cups cake flour
¼ tsp. Kosher salt

3 cups sugar
1 cup sour cream
1 oz. Gran Marnier
½ tsp. baking soda

Cream butter and sugar together until fluffy. Add sour cream and eggs, scrape bowl and mix orange juice, zest and liquer into batter. Sift together cake flour, baking soda & salt. Beat dry ingredients gently into batter until smooth. Fold 2½ cups fresh cranberries into orange batter. Liberally grease a tube pan and fill with batter. Bake at 325° for an hour or until knife inserted halfway from center comes out clean. Cool in the pan.

<u>GRANZEST GLAZE</u>

In a small saucepan over medium heat combine 2½ cups sugar, one oz. Gran Marnier, zest of one large orange and ¼ cup water. Cook until mixture boils, stirring occasionally. Whisk in ¼ cup cold butter, cut into small pieces, until thoroughly combined. Pour into container and cool until set. Remove cake from tube pan and place on serving plate. Pour cooled mixture over cake.

Locklear's Lowcountry Grill

Mt. Pleasant and Charleston

CAJUN SHRIMP & GRITS

2 lbs. shrimp, peeled & deveined
1½ cups green onions, washed & sliced
3 cups mushrooms, cleaned & sliced
1 tbsp. blackened spice
1 cup tomato jam (available at Locklear's)

3 cups heavy cream
2 tbsp. Dijon mustard
6 ct. corn fritters (1 per plate)
1½ cups cooked grits

In a large sauté pan start the heavy cream on medium to high heat and add the mushrooms, onions, mustard and spice. Allow to cook until the cream just starts to thicken and add the shrimp. Prepare your hot serving plates with the grits and 1 corn fritter per plate topped with jam. When the shrimp are just done spoon mixture over grits.

Tomato jam is optional for topping the corn fritters, and one could substitute another jam readily available if desired.

Lowndes Grove Plantation
266 St. Margaret Street
Charleston

PEANUT BUTTER & BANANA FRENCH TOAST

¼ cup cool water
2 bananas, peeled, sliced into ½" chunks
½ tsp. vanilla extract
4 slices egg bread (challah)

1 tbsp. margarine
3 eggs, beaten
2 tsp. peanut butter
2 tbsp. real maple syrup

In a shallow bowl (like a soup bowl) beat water and vanilla into eggs until well mixed. Spread a teaspoon of peanut butter onto two slices of bread and dip into egg mixture. Then take the other two slices and dip them into egg mixture. Heat margarine in a large frying pan over medium heat. When margarine starts bubbling, add the peanut butter slices into the skillet with the peanut butter side up.

Quickly lay out banana pieces (saving some for garnish) onto the peanut butter and top with a slice of egg-dipped bread. Squish the sandwich together with a spatula. Let cook for about 3 minutes on first side and then cook for another few minutes on the other side. After 6 or 7 minutes of cooking, if sandwich seems too moist, cover pan with a lid and let cook an additional minute or two. Turn out the French toast sandwiches onto big plates, topped with a few thoughtfully placed banana slices. Serve with maple syrup.

Magnolia's
185 E. Bay Street
Charleston

CREAM CHEESE BROWNIE

8 oz. sweet chocolate
6 oz. butter
6 oz. cream cheese, softened
1 cup English walnuts, chopped
¼ tsp. almond extract

1 tbsp. vanilla
1 tsp. baking powder
½ tsp. salt
2 cups sugar
6 eggs

1¼ cups flour

Melt the chocolate with 3 oz. of the butter over a double boiler, remove and let cool to room temperature. Cream the remaining 3 oz. of butter with the cream cheese. Gradually add ½ cup sugar, then blend in 2 eggs, 2 tbsp. flour and 1 tbsp. vanilla. Set aside.

Beat 4 eggs until opaque, gradually add the 1½ cups remaining sugar and baking powder mixed together, then add salt and remaining flour. Stir in melted chocolate mixture. Add nuts and rest of vanilla extract and almond extract. Pour chocolate batter into a greased 8x12 cake pan and fold in the cream cheese batter. Bake at 350° 35-40 minutes.

McCrady's
2 Unity Alley
Charleston

HEART OF PALM SALAD WITH CANDIED WALNUTS & CRUMBLED GOAT CHEESE

12 oz. mixed baby lettuce   4 oz. candied walnuts
4 oz. goat cheese, crumbled   salt & pepper to taste
8 oz. fresh Heart of Palm, cut 3" x ¼" batons

Place 4 batons of Heart of Palm on the plate. Add crumbled goat cheese and candied walnuts around. Drizzle a little walnut vinaigrette around plate. Toss the baby lettuce with the remainder of the vinaigrette and season with salt & pepper. Place greens equally in the middle of the plate.

WALNUT VINAIGRETTE

1 tsp. dijon mustard ¼ cup walnut oil   1/8 cup canola oil
2 tbsp. red wine vinegar   2 tbsp. honey

Mix ingredients well in a small mixing bowl. Serve over heart of palm salad.

Middleton Place
4300 Ashley River Road
Charleston

CORN PUDDING

2 cups yellow corn
2 whole eggs
¾ qt. heavy cream

¼ tsp. nutmeg
pinch of salt & white pepper

Place yellow corn in a greased casserole pan. Mix all other ingredients together. Pour mixture over corn and bake for 45 minutes at 350° or until golden brown.

Mistral Mistral Mistral Restaurant
99 South Market Street
Charleston

ROASTED PORK LOIN WITH CALVADOES CREME & NEW POTATOES

1¾ lb. pork loin
2 red delicious apples, chopped & cored
2 oz. Calvadoes or other apple brandy
1 tsp. garlic
2 tbsp. butter
2 tbsp. butter

2 large leeks
3 tbsp. honey
12-15 Red Bliss potatoes
1 cup heavy cream
1 tsp. olive oil
salt & pepper

Rub pork loin with salt and pepper. Roast in a slow oven (275°) for about 2 hours. Rest until service.

Cut potatoes in half and put in bowl and toss with garlic and olive oil. Roast in oven at same temperature for 45 minutes or until soft. Hold.

In large skillet sauté leeks in butter until soft. Add apple, honey & brandy. This will flame. Cook 4-6 minutes or until reduced by half. Add cream, cook for 4 minutes or until desired consistency. Slice the pork thin and serve sauce over with potatoes to the side.

MOUSAKA - Greek Eggplant Casserole

1½ lbs. ground beef
4 tbsp. butter
¼ tsp. pepper
5 medium zucchini
grated Romano cheese

chopped parsley
1½ tsp. salt
8 medium potatoes
2 chopped onions
vegetable oil

1 clove minced garlic
2 medium eggplants
1 tsp. sugar
1 cup tomato sauce

Add garlic, salt & pepper to ground beef. Cook slowly until meat is done. Add chopped onions, parsley & butter. Brown well. Add tomato sauce, sugar and one cup water. Simmer until thickened, about 15 minutes.

Slice eggplants, potatoes, and zucchini. Fry or brush with oil and broil until golden. In a 9" x 13" baking pan begin layering potatoes, then zucchini, and last eggplant. Pour meat sauce evenly over vegetables. Top with a layer of cream sauce (see below). Sprinkle liberally with grated cheese. Bake for 30 minutes at 350°. Makes 10-12 servings.

CREAM SAUCE
6 tbsp. butter • 3 cups milk • 6 tbsp. flour • 5 egg yolks

Melt butter. Add flour and stir until light brown. Add milk gradually, stirring constantly until slightly thickened. Slowly add egg yolks and cook over very low heat until thick. Season with salt and pepper to taste.

Old Village Post House
101 Pitt Street
Mt. Pleasant

GAZPACHO

2 cups red wine vinegar
1/3 cup garlic
6 red bell peppers, finely diced
Stalks from 1 head celery, finely diced
12 cucumbers, peeled & finely diced

¼ cup salt
3 red onions, finely diced
3 qts. chopped tomatoes
2 cups tomato paste
4 qts. water

GARNISH

Cracked black pepper

Fresh mint, chopped

Macerate onions and garlic in red wine vinegar. Dissolve tomato paste in water. Add all remaining ingredients. Garnish with cracked black pepper and fresh chopped mint.

Oscars
207 W. 5th Street North
Summerville

BANANAS OSCAR

1 ripe banana, sliced lengthwise and halved
4 tbsp. rum (light)
4 tbsp. banana liqueur
4 tbsp. brown sugar

3 tbsp. butter
4 scoops vanilla ice cream
4 tbsp. candied pecans (optional)
whipped cream (optional)

Combine rum and next 3 ingredients in a sauté pan over medium heat. Bring to a simmer and add sliced banana. Cook briefly on each side keep warm.

CAROLINA TROUT WITH LITTLENECK CLAMS & A CITRUS SAFFRONETTE

1 onion, chopped	4 garlic cloves, crushed
1 cup orange juice	1 cup champagne vinegar
pinch saffron	2 tsp. dijon mustard
2 cups extra virgin olive oil	1 cup vegetable oil
4 Carolina trout filets	12 Littleneck clams
6 artichokes, braised	8 baby carrots, steamed
16 asparagus, steamed	2 blood oranges, segmented

salt & sugar to taste

Combine the onions, garlic, orange juice, vinegar and saffron in a pan. Slowly simmer until reduced by half. Place in a blender and mix until smooth. Add the mustard and slowly add the oils. Strain. Season with salt and sugar.

In a hot pan, sear the trout on both sides until golden brown and crispy. Reserve. In another pan, steam the clams until they open. Reserve.

Heat vegetables and saffronette. Place in the bottom of a bowl. Place the trout on top of them and the clams and orange segments around the perimeter of the bowl.

Peninsula Grill
112 N. Market Street
Charleston

LOW COUNTRY STUFFED QUAIL WITH OYSTER-LEEK RAGOUT & HOMINY GRITS CAKE

12 Quail (2 per serving plate)
¼ cup onion, brunoise
1 cup cornbread, crumbled
1 cup chicken stock
salt & pepper

¼ cup bacon, smoked, diced, small
¼ cup celery, brunoise
1 cup toasted pecans
¼ cup melted butter

In medium saucepan, render bacon over medium heat until bacon is crisp. Remove bacon, leaving rendered drippings in pan. Set bacon aside. In same pan as bacon, sweat onions and celery until translucent. Set aside.

In medium bowl combine onions, celery and reserved bacon with cornbread, pecans and melted butter. Pour enough chicken stock to bind all ingredients so that stuffing can be formed into balls and hold their shape. Stuff each quail with stuffing - approximately 1½ tbsp. per quail. Season each quail with salt & pepper. Sear quail and place in oven at 450°. Cook for 5-7 minutes or until desired doneness is achieved. In large sauté pan, sauté spinach in 2 tbsp. brown butter until just wilted. Season with salt & pepper.

Poogan's Porch
72 Queen Street
Charleston

POOGAN'S PEANUT BUTTER PIE

1 8oz. pkg. cream cheese	1 cup powdered sugar
¾ cup creamy or chunky peanut butter	1 tsp. vanilla
½ cup whipping cream, whipped	1-9" baked pie crust

Beat cream cheese until soft & fluffy. Beat in sugar, peanut butter & vanilla. Slowly fold in whipped cream until well blended. Pour into baked pie crust and freeze until ready to serve. Remove from freezer and let soften 20 to 30 minutes before serving.

Rice Hope Plantation
206 Rice Hope Drive
Moncks Corner

AGNE'S SUNRISE PLEASER

2 lbs. sausage, cooked & drained
4 eggs, beaten
1 (6-oz.) pkg. cornbread mix
½ cup butter, melted

½ lb. grated cheese
1 cup cooked grits
1½ cups milk, heated
¾ tsp. salt

Grease 9" x 13" baking dish. Layer sausage and ½ of the cheese on bottom of dish. Mix eggs and next 5 ingredients. Pour over sausage mixture and top with remaining cheese. Refrigerate overnight. Bring to room temperature. Bake at 350° for 45 to 60 minutes. Check center for doneness with a toothpick.

Robert's
182 East Bay Street
Charleston

ROBERT'S SPICY BAKED SHRIMP

1 lb. raw large shrimp, rinsed in cold water
2 tbsp. <u>Robert's Original Seasoning</u>
1 lemon, cut into wedges
4 cloves garlic, pressed or minced

2 tbsp. fresh lemon juice
1 tbsp. honey
½ cup olive oil
1 tbsp. soy sauce

In a 2 quart baking dish combine lemon juice, garlic, Robert's Seasoning, oil, honey & soy sauce. Add shrimp (do not remove shells), toss to coat thoroughly. Refrigerate at least 1 hour. Preheat outdoor grill or oven to 450°. Bake or grill shrimp until cooked through, about 8 to 10 minutes. Garnish with lemon wedges.

Rose Bank Farms Cafe

Bohicket Marina Village
Johns Island

PUMPKIN PIE

CRUST

1½ cups graham cracker crumbs   4 oz. butter

Mix ingredients together and place in a tall cake pan. Bake at 375° for 8-10 minutes. Let crust cool to room temperature.

15 oz. pumpkin (canned is acceptable)   ½ cup granulated sugar
1 cup firmly packed brown sugar   4 whole eggs
¼ cup evaporated milk   3 tbsp. flour
2 tsp. pumpkin pie spice   ½ tsp. ground cinnamon
24 oz. cream cheese

Beat cream cheese and sugar until soft and fluffy. Add the other ingredients and mix thoroughly. Bake in preheated oven at 325° for 1½ hours.

Saltwater Grill
2213 B. Middle Street
Sullivans Island

RICE FRITTERS

6 cups Jasamine rice - cooked & chilled
6 cups Carolina gold rice - cooked & chilled

1 cup diced peppers	1 cup cream
1 tbsp. chopped thyme	5 egg yolks
hot chili sauce to taste	salt & pepper to taste

rice flour - add to adjust consistency

Mix all above ingredients. Form into small balls. Drop into hot grease (like hushpuppies) and fry crispy brown.

Sea Biscuit Cafe
21 JC Long Boulevard
Isle of Palms

BANANA BREAD

1½ cups all purpose flour
1½ tsp. baking powder
1½ cup over-ripe bananas, mashed
½ cup melted butter or margarine

1½ tsp. baking soda
2 eggs
1 tbsp. vanilla extract
¾ cup sugar

Mix dry ingredients together in a bowl. Mix wet ingredients together, and blend in the dry ingredients. Bake in a well greased loaf pan at 400° for 10 minutes. Then turn oven to 350° and bake for another 45 minutes. Makes one loaf.

Sermet's Corner
276 King Street
Charleston

COLD CUCUMBER & DILL SOUP

2 lbs. plain yogurt
8 oz. sour cream
3-4 peeled, seeded cucumbers
1-2 cups water (as desired)
salt & pepper to taste

1 tsp. fresh chopped garlic
3 oz. olive oil
1 bunch fresh dill
1 bunch fresh mint

Finely chop cucumber, dill & mint. Add garlic, sour cream, yogurt; mix well. Blend in oil, salt & pepper and water to desired consistency. Chill and serve.

Slightly North of Broad
192 East Bay Street
Charleston

SHRIMP BISQUE WITH THAI CURRY & BLUE CRAB CLAW MEAT

2 yellow onions, medium size, medium dice
2 large carrots, medium dice
3 red bell peppers, medium dice
1 head fennel bulb or ½ head celery, medium dice
1½ - 2 cups all purpose flour
4 qts. strong shrimp stock
1 lb. blue crab claw meat, cleaned

1 tbsp. salt
¾ lb. butter
1 tbsp. red Thai curry
1 qt. cream
1 tbsp. Tabasco
1 cup Madeira
1 tsp. white pepper

Melt butter in sauté pan. Add salt, then add all vegetables. Sweat until tender. Add curry paste and stir. Add flour to vegetables and stir, making a roux. Whisk in shrimp stock, then simmer 10-15 minutes. Whisk in cream and simmer 5 minutes. Sauté crab meat in butter, then add to bisque. Add Tabasco, Madeira, and white pepper, stirring to mix. Check seasoning level.

Starfish Grille
101 E. Artic Avenue
Folly Beach
SHRIMP ETOUFFÉE AND GRITS

1 cup cheddar cheese, grated	½ lb. butter
½ lb. plain flour	1 bay leaf
pinch thyme leaf	pinch salt
Cajun seasoning to taste	1 tsp. black pepper
1 red pepper, chopped	1 large onion
1 green pepper, chopped	1 tbsp. chopped garlic
3 ribs celery	1 cup white wine
3 cups shrimp stock	stone ground grits (cooked)
1 cup parmesan cheese, grated	2 lbs. shrimp

Make brown roux out of butter and flour. Sauté peppers, onions, celery and garlic in butter until tender. Add white wine and reduce by half. Add shrimp stock and remaining ingredients. Stir constantly until thickens. You may need to add a little white roux. Add cooked shrimp at the end. Place stone ground grits in dish and top with grated cheddar cheese. Serve with Shrimp Etoufée over the grits and top with parmesan cheese.

Station 22
2205 Middle Street
Sullivan's Island

PAN SEARED BLACK GROUPER OVER CREAMY CLEMSON BLUE CHEESE GRITS WITH A BACON ROCK SHRIMP TOMATO BROTH

2 oz. Clemson Blue Cheese crumbles
2 oz. diced bacon
1 tsp. chopped shallots
4 oz. diced tomato concasse
2 scallions
kosher salt & black pepper to taste

1 serving cooked grits
1 tsp. chopped garlic
4 oz. chicken stock
1 oz. butter
1 tbsp. olive oil

Make your favorite grits (preferably yellow stone ground). When finished, add blue cheese crumbles and hold on low heat. In a medium sauté pan heat olive oil on high heat. Season grouper filet with kosher salt and black pepper. Place grouper in sauté pan and sear both sides. Remove from pan and finish in oven on 350° for about 8 to 12 minutes. Place bacon in same sauté pan and render. Add shallots and garlic. Be careful not to burn. Deglaze pan with chicken stock. Add diced tomato concasse. Add whole unsalted butter.

Place grits in medium to large bowl. Place fish on top of grits. With a spoon place ingredients on grouper. Pour sauce around grouper. Garnish with julienne scallions.

Sticky Fingers Restaurant & Bar

Charleston, Mt. Pleasant, North Charleston, Summerville

SAVANNAH DIP

2-10 oz. packages frozen Stouffer's cream spinach
1½ cups shredded mozzarella cheese
½ can cream of mushroom soup
1 cup artichoke hearts, quartered
½ tsp. garlic powder

Thaw spinach. Combine all ingredients in a bowl and mix. Bake in a 9" x 9" casserole dish at 375° for 20 minutes. Serve with a side of salsa and nacho chips.

St. Andrew's Parish Church
Highway 61, Ashley River Road
Charleston

ASHLEY RIVER MUD CAKE

2 sticks butter or margarine	1 tsp. baking soda
4 tbsp. cocoa	½ tsp. salt
1 cup water	½ cup buttermilk
2 cups sugar	2 eggs
2 cups flour	1 tsp. vanilla

Melt the butter or margarine and add the cocoa and water. Bring to a boil. Mix the sugar, flour, baking soda and salt together in a medium bowl. Add the chocolate mixture and stir with a wire whisk. Add buttermilk, eggs and vanilla. Mix well and pour into greased jelly roll pan. Bake at 350° for 20 minutes.

ICING

1 stick butter or margarine	1 box 4 X sugar
4 tbsp. cocoa	½ cup nuts
6 tbsp. buttermilk	1 tbsp. vanilla

Make the icing while the cake bakes. Melt the butter or margarine and add the cocoa and buttermilk. Bring to a boil and add the remaining ingredients, while stirring. Put icing on cake while still warm. You can make, bake, frost and have the cake ready to eat in less than an hour.

Sunfire Grill & Bistro
1090 Sam Rittenburg Boulevard
Charleston

PEACH PERFECTION

6 fresh peaches, peeled, pitted & sliced very thin

6 oz. sugar

½ oz. peach schnapps

Graham cracker crumbs

mint for garnish

6 oz. egg yolks

1 oz. Michele Chiario Nivolle

1 cup heavy cream

Combine sugar and egg yolks in a double boiler and whisk until the mixture has doubled in volume. The mixture should be thick enough to draw a figure eight with the whisk before it dissipates. Once the consistency is achieved, immediately cool it over an ice bath.

Whip the heavy cream to a stiff peak and gently fold it into the egg/sugar mixture. Flavor the mixture with the schnapps and the Nivolle. The rest of the dessert can be presented either individually in wine or parfait glasses, or it can be presented in a large, clear glass bowl. Fill the serving container with the sliced peaches on the bottom. Cover the peaches with a generous layer of graham cracker crumbs. Spoon in the peach cream. Garnish with a few slices of peaches and a few sprigs of mint. Chill for about an hour before serving.

Sunny Meadows Bed & Breakfast
1459 Venning Road
Mt. Pleasant

HOUSTON'S ROSEBUD FARMS FRUIT DISH

5-6 golden delicious apples
1 (16 oz.) can cranberry sauce (whole berries)
1 (8 oz.) can crushed pineapple, drained

Peel, core and dice apples. Add cranberry sauce and pineapple. Pour into a 9 x 13 inch baking dish; cover and refrigerate overnight. Bring to room temperature.

TOPPING

¼ cup flour
1/3 cup brown sugar
½ cup raw oatmeal

½ tsp. cinnamon
¼ cup butter

Mix all topping ingredients and sprinkle on top of fruit. Bake at 350° for 45 minutes. Serve hot or cold.

Swamp Fox Restaurant & Bar
387 King Street
Charleston

PEACH BOURBON GLAZE

3 lbs. peaches, peeled & pitted	3 lbs. onion (¼ chopped)
¼ cup cider vinegar	¼ cup molasses
4 cups bourbon	¼ lb. brown sugar
1 tbsp. garlic	4 qts. veal stock

Caramelize onions and add garlic with peaches. Cook for 45 minutes, deglaze with bourbon and reduce until pan is almost dry.

Add remaining ingredients. Reduce entire volume by 1/3 and purée. Allow to simmer for approximately 20 more minutes. Season with salt and pepper. Cool.

T-Bonz Gill & Grill
West Ashley, Mt. Pleasant & Charleston

ISLAND MARINATED SIRLOIN STEAKS

23 oz. pineapple juice	½ cup teriyaki sauce
5 oz. brown sugar	1 oz. chopped garlic
1 cup diced yellow onions	½ tbsp. ground ginger

Place all ingredients in a mixing bowl and whisk until thoroughly mixed. Make sure all steaks are completely immersed. Cover and refrigerate. Steaks must marinate for 48 hours to achieve desired flavor and tenderness. After a maximum of 72 hours, the steaks must be removed from the marinade or the meat will become mushy from over-marination. Grill and enjoy.

CREAMY SHRIMP & GRITS

CREAMY GRITS

1 cup water	1 cup half & half or whole milk
2 oz. butter	¾ cup quick grits
salt & white pepper to taste	

In a small saucepan combine the water, milk and butter. Add salt. Bring to a simmer and add the grits. Cook over medium low heat for 10-15 minutes until grits are tender. Add white pepper to taste. Cooked grits should have the same consistency as oatmeal or Cream of Wheat.

CREAMY CHARLESTON SHRIMP

4 strips of bacon, sliced into ¼" pieces	3 colves of garlic, minced
1 lb. peeled & deveined small shrimp	¼ cup flour
2 peeled, seeded & diced medium tomatoes	1½ cups half & half
8 thinly sliced scallions, keep the white & green parts separated	
salt & cayenne or white pepper to taste	

Cook bacon until crisp in a sauté pan. Add shrimp, scallion whites & garlic to the bacon and grease. Sauté until shrimp just begins to firm up. Dust the mixture with flour and stir until well blended. Add tomatoes and half and half. Stir until well blended. Bring to a simmer, stirring occasionally. Season with salt & pepper to taste. Serve immediately over grits or rice. Garnish with the remaining scallion greens. Excellent accompaniments are crisp bacon slices and fresh sliced beef steak tomatoes.

The Boathouse
101 Palm Boulevard, Isle of Palms
& 549 E. Bay Street, Charleston

BOATHOUSE BLEU CHEESE COLESLAW

COLESLAW

2 heads green cabbage
crumbled bleu cheese, to taste

½ red onion, chopped
1 carrot, shredded

DRESSING

4 cups mayonnaise
1 cup half & half
¼ cup olive oil
cayenne pepper, to taste

1½ cups sour cream
½ cup balsamic vinegar
salt, to taste

In a large bowl combine cabbage, carrot, onion, and bleu cheese. In another large bowl stir together mayonnaise, sour cream, half & half, balsamic vinegar, olive oil, salt & pepper. Keep stirring until blended together thoroughly. Pour dressing over the slaw ingredients and mix well until evenly distributed.

The Crab Shack
1901 Ashley River Road
Charleston

LOW COUNTRY BOIL

½ - 1 cup Old Bay seasoning   1 lemon, cut in half
1 lime, cut in half   1 onion, cut in quarters
3 lbs. new potatoes, cut in half   5 ears corn, cut in thirds
2 lbs. sausage, cut in 2 inch chunks   10 blue crabs, alive
50 Small Neck or Cherry Stone clams, closed and scrubbed
3 lbs. shrimp, 31-35 count

In an extra large stock pot (30-60 qt.) with straining basket, fill with water to 3 inches from top. Add ½ - 1 cup Old Bay, lemon, lime and onion. Add any veggie scraps you may have (celery, carrots, etc.). Boil on low for 1 hour. You may need additional water at this point. Add new potatoes and bring back to boil. When potatoes are fork tender add corn, sausage, blue crab and clams. Bring to boil and cook for approximately 3 minutes or until clams start to open. Add shrimp and cook 2 more minutes. Carefully pull basket and dump on table. Shake Old Bay over all of it. Retain stock for additional boils that day.

The Variety Store
Municipal Yacht Basin
17 Lockwood Drive, Charleston

KEY LIME PIE

6 egg yolks, beaten slightly
1 can sweetened condensed milk
½ cup lime juice
6 tbsp. sugar

1 9-inch baked pie shell
6 egg whites
½ tsp. cream of tartar

Preheat oven to 300°. Combine egg yolks, condensed milk and lime juice. Blend well. Pour into baked pie shell. Beat egg whites until frothy. Add cream of tartar and continue to beat until stiff. Gradually add sugar and beat until meringue is stiff and glossy. Swirl onto top of pie. Bake in oven until meringue is golden brown.

Tommy Conclon's
160 Church Street
Charleston

IRISH COFFEE

freshly brewed piping hot coffee   1 jigger Irish whiskey
2 tsp. dark brown sugar   chilled fresh whipped cream

Heat the whiskey and sugar. Preheat the glass or cup. Dip the glass rim in the liquor before pouring in the whiskey and sugar. Fill to the top with coffee and stir. Top with whipped cream and serve immediately.

LOBSTER SAUCE

¼ lb. butter
½ cup shallots, diced
½ cup garlic, diced
½ cup brandy

1 cup all-purpose flour
lobster stock (from recipe)
½ qt. heavy cream, 36% milk fat
salt & white pepper to taste

Melt butter in stock pot and add shallots and garlic; sauté until translucent. Deglaze with brandy and slowly add flour to pan to create roux. Add enough flour so that a spoon cleans bottom of pan. Cook roux until proper consistency is achieved over low heat. Slowly add stock in 4 parts to ensure no roux balls form. Bring to a simmer to cook out roux and add heavy cream. Check seasoning to ensure proper flavor has been achieved. Strain liquid through china cap to get rid of any by-product.

Tristan
55 South Market Street, Charleston

CREAM OF SWEET CORN SOUP WITH "MUDBUGS" & SMOKED BACON

6 ears sweet corn (shucked)
½ lb. smoked bacon, diced
2 tsps. chopped chives (optional garnish)
20 whole black peppercorns
freshly ground black pepper

30 crawfish
5 bay leaves
sea salt
12 oz. cream base

Cook the shucked corn in rapidly boiling salted water for 5 minutes. Cool in ice water and remove the kernels from the cob. Puree the corn in a food processor. Fill a large pot 2/3 full with water. Put in bay leaves, black peppercorns and a small handful of sea salt. Bring the water to a boil. Add the crawfish and return to a boil for 3 minutes. Let stand for 3 minutes. Strain the crawfish and immediately cool in an ice bath. When cool, pick the meat, and devein. Cook bacon until crisp, and drain on paper towels. In a soup pot add corn puree and cream base. When hot adjust seasoning. In 6 bowls divide crawfish, bacon and chives. Ladle hot soup on top and serve.

CREAM BASE

1 large onion, diced
1 cup dry white wine
2 cups heavy cream

4 shallots, sliced
2 cups chicken stock

Cook the onion and shallots with a bit of olive oil until they are clear. Add the white wine and reduce until almost dry. Add the chicken stock and reduce until almost dry. Add the cream and reduce slowly for 10 minutes. Strain.

Two Meeting Street
2 Meeting Street
Charleston

CUCUMBER SPREAD

1 8oz. pkg. cream cheese
1 stick butter
1 medium cucumber, peeled, seeded & grated
½ tsp. garlic powder

Combine all above ingredients. Place in a small glass bowl and serve with crackers or assorted vegetables.

Vickery's
Charleston & Mt. Pleasant
BLACK BEAN CAKES

1-16oz. can black beans, cooked
1 large red onion, diced
1 tsp. red pepper flakes
1 tsp. chili powder
salt & pepper to taste
sautéed spinach
16 oz. fresh, finely ground breadcrumbs
salsa

1 large green pepper, diced
1 red bell pepper, diced
1 tbsp. cumin
1 tbsp. granulated garlic
olive oil
balsamic vinegar
1 egg
sour cream

Drain and wash cooked black beans. Let dry completely. Dice greens, peppers, large red onion, red bell pepper and blot dry. Mix beans, peppers and onion together in a mixing bowl. Season with crushed red pepper flakes, cumin, chili powder, granulated garlic, salt and pepper. Whip egg. Combine with bean mix and toss with breadcrumbs. Refrigerate for 1 hour to set, then mold into patties. Pan sauté in little olive oil and serve over sautéed spinach, red onions and a dash of balsamic vinegar. Top with salsa and sour cream.

Vista Riverside Grill

360 Concord Street, Ste. 111
Charleston

TUNA TARTAR

1 lb. tuna, small, dice
3 tsp. fresh ginger, minced
2 tsp. Wasabi paste
¼ cup soy sauce

1 cup green onions, minced
2 tsp. garlic, minced
1½ tsp. sesame oil
lime juice (½ lime)

Combine all and serve on sesame wafers or gaufrette chips.

Waters Edge
Mt. Pleasant

OYSTER BREADING

12 cups Jap. bread crumbs	3 cups Asiago
3 tbsp. oregano	2 tbsp. thyme
3 tbsp. kosher salt	2 tbsp. coarse ground pepper
½ cup parsley, chopped	.6 cup clarified butter

Place this breading mixture on top of oysters on the half shell and bake at 350° until light brown crust forms.

ALONG THE BATTERY
LEMONADE ICE CREAM

1 6oz. can frozen lemonade concentrate, thawed and diluted
as directed on can

1 qt. half & half   2 tbsp. vanilla extract

2 14oz. cans sweetened condensed milk

Combine all ingredients. Pour mixture into a freezer can of a one gallon electric freezer. Freeze according to manufacturer's instructions.

ASHLEY'S BAKED TOMATO HALVES

6 large tomatoes

12 tbsp. butter, divided in ½

½ cup finely chopped onion

2 tsp. prepared mustard

1 tsp. Worcestershire sauce

6 tsp. chopped parsley

6 slices bread, torn into coarse crumbs

Preheat oven to 350°. Wash tomatoes, remove stems and cut in half crosswise. Put tomatoes, cut side up, in baking dish. Sauté onion in 6 tbsp. butter until tender. Put this mixture on tomatoes. Melt remaining butter and add crumbs and parsley. Sprinkle this mixture over tomatoes. Bake for 20 minutes until golden brown.

BESS'S PECAN THINS

1 large stick butter, softened   ½ cup brown sugar
½ cup chopped pecans   ½ cup white sugar
1 tsp. vanilla   1½ cups flour
¼ tsp. baking powder   ¼ tsp. baking soda
1 small egg

Put all ingredients in a bowl except the egg. Mix for 5 minutes by hand, then add the egg. Keep mixing until you can form a log with the dough measuring about 1½ inches in diameter. Roll the log in wax paper and chill overnight.

Slice cold dough into 1/8" thick cookies. Space about 1 inch apart on a greased pan. Bake 12 minutes. Remove cookies from pan while warm.

CANDY STORE PRALINES

2 cups sugar	1 cup buttermilk
2 tsp. light corn syrup	2 tsp. butter
1 tsp. baking soda	1 tsp. vanilla
1 cup coarse broken pecans	

Line a large cookie sheet with wax paper. In a heavy saucepan stir together the sugar, buttermilk, syrup, butter and baking soda. Soda will cause mixture to bubble slightly. Stir constantly. Cook over low heat until it comes to a boil. Continue stirring for 5 more minutes until a candy thermometer reaches 238° or a small amount of the mixture dropped into very cold water forms a soft ball. Remove from heat and cool 2 minutes. Add vanilla and beat until it loses its gloss. Add nuts and drop immediately on wax paper.

CARRIAGE ROW TEA CAKES

4 cups all purpose flour	2 eggs
1¼ cups sugar	¾ cup butter
1 tsp. vanilla	

Cream butter and sugar. Add all other ingredients and continue to cream. Roll into a ball about the size of a small egg.

Preheat oven. Put the ball of dough on a greased cookie sheet and pat it to about one inch thick. Bake at 325° for 15 to 20 minutes.

CHARLESTON RED RICE

¼ lb. bacon, chopped
1/3 cup green peppers, chopped
1 8oz. can tomato sauce
1 cup uncooked white rice

½ cup onions, chopped
1 cup water
1 tsp. brown sugar
¼ tsp. salt

Sauté bacon, onions and green peppers until tender. Add water, tomato sauce, brown sugar and salt. Bring to a boil and add the rice. Reduce heat, cover and simmer for 20 minutes.

CHART HOUSE SHRIMP RÉMOULADE

1 pkg. crab boil
3 tbsp. salt

1 gallon water
2 lbs. shrimp

In a large pot bring the water to a full boil. Add the shrimp. When the water returns to a boil, turn the heat off and allow the shrimp to sit and absorb the seasonings. Drain the shrimp, let them cool and peel them before serving.

RÉMOULADE SAUCE

1 cup ketchup
2 tsp. Worcestershire sauce
4 hard boiled eggs, chopped
2 raw eggs, beaten

2 tbsp. horseradish
2 tbsp. yellow mustard
dash Tabasco

Mix all ingredients until well blended. Chill the sauce before serving.

CHRISTMAS CRANBERRY CRUNCH

1 lb. cranberries   2 cups sugar
2 cups water

Let these 3 ingredients come to a boil in a heavy pot. Cranberries will start popping. Cook about 10 minutes. Add:

1 cup raisins   ¾ tsp. allspice

Reduce heat and let simmer for about 10 minutes. Add:

1 cup chopped walnuts   1 tsp. Worchestershire sauce

Stir. Let mixture cool down until it thickens, about 5 to 10 minutes. Fill 4 pint jars. Keep refrigerated.

CHURCH STREET SALMON

2-6 oz. salmon filets
4 slices mozzarella cheese
8 stalks asparagus, blanched
4 tbsp. fresh parsley, chopped

6 strips bacon
2 tsp. garlic
2 tbsp. Madiera wine
salt & pepper to taste

Slice each salmon filet horizontally. Between each layer place 2 slices of cheese and 4 stalks asparagus. Wrap each filet with 3 slices of bacon. Place the salmon filets in a hot pan, seam side down. Sear each side of the filets until bacon is golden. Place pan in 350° oven for 1 hour and 15 minutes.

Remove filets from pan and keep warm. Pour bacon grease out of the pan and sauté the garlic. Deglaze with the wine and reduce by half. Add cream and reduce by half. Season sauce with salt and pepper, and add parsley. Pour sauce on warm plate, top with salmon filet and serve.

CONFEDERATE BEAN SOUP

1 cup onion, chopped	½ quart water
1 cup celery, chopped	2/3 cup brown sugar
1 cup bacon, chopped	1 quart can baked beans
1-3 cups Hillshire Farms sausage, sliced	1 quart heavy cream

Sauté the onion, celery and bacon. When the onion is translucent, pour off fat. Pour all ingredients into a large pot and stir. Bring mixture to a boil and serve.

EXCHANGE STREET POPPY SEED DRESSING

¾ cup sugar
1 tsp. salt
1 tbsp. onion juice
1 tbsp. poppy seed

1 tbsp. dry mustard
1/3 cup cider vinegar
1 cup salad oil

Mix sugar, mustard, salt & vinegar. Add onion juice. At medium speed slowly add oil. Beat well until thick. Add poppy seed. Makes one pint. Keep in refrigerator. Great for fruit salads or over baked ham.

FARMERS MARKET SOUP

1 onion, diced
1 clove garlic, chopped
2 cucumbers, skinned, seeded & diced
3 ribs celery, diced
6 medium tomatoes, seeded & diced

1 cup red wine vinegar
2 cups cooked butter beans
2 cups cooked corn
2 cups tomato juice
Tabasco to taste

Marinate onions with vinegar and garlic for 1 hour. Add remaining ingredients. Serve chilled in soup bowl. Garnish with a dollop of sour cream.

FRENCH-STYLE GREEN BEANS

1 tbsp. butter	½ lb. diced country ham
½ large onion, finely chopped	2 cups water
6 small new potatoes	1 tsp. salt
3 lbs. string beans	¼ tsp. black pepper

Melt the butter in a saucepan. Add ham and cook for 5 minutes. Add the onion and sauté until it becomes translucent. Add potatoes and water. Cover and cook for 10 minutes. Add string beans, salt and pepper, and cook 25 minutes more over medium heat.

FRIED OKRA PATTIES

2 lbs. fresh okra

1 cup milk

salt & pepper to taste

2 cups self rising flour (to coat)

Cut the okra crosswise, not too thin. Drop the okra in a bowl of milk for a few minutes, drain, salt & pepper. Then sprinkle flour over it. Drop large spoonfuls into hot cooking oil (about medium heat). Turn over when one side is golden brown, and brown other side. Remove with a spatula and drain on paper towels.

GRASSHOPPER PIE

4 tbsp. Creme de Menthe (green)	1 cup cream, whipped
2 tbsp. Creme de Cocoa (white)	1 baked pie crust
2 cups tiny marshmallows	

Melt marshmallows in a double boiler, cool. Add flavorings, fold in cream. Add green coloring, if needed. Put in pie shell and refrigerate.

LOW COUNTRY CREAM OF BROCCOLI SOUP

2 cups onion, sliced thin	2 tbsp. butter
4 cups broccoli (chopped, all woody parts removed)	
2 tbsp. flour	1 quart milk
1 cup potatoes, peeled & diced	2¼ tsp. salt
1 cup heavy whipping cream	½ tsp. pepper

Sauté the onions in the butter until they are soft - not brown. Add broccoli and cook for 10 minutes. Sprinkle flour over the vegetables and stir. Add milk, potatoes, salt & pepper. Cook for 20 minutes on low heat. Puree the soup in a blender. Put back into a saucepan and add the cream. Reheat slowly and serve.

MEETING STREET BLUE CHEESE DRESSING

1 cup sour cream	½ tsp. dry mustard
½ tsp. black pepper	½ tsp. salt
½ tsp. garlic powder	1½ cups mayonnaise
1 tsp. Worchestershire sauce	¾ cup Danish blue cheese

Combine all ingredients except the blue cheese in a large mixing bowl. Beat with an electric mixer for 2 minutes at a low speed. Crumble cheese and add to mixture. Blend at a low speed for a couple of minutes. Chill in refrigerator for several hours.

MY FABULOUS FIG JAM

Stem and scald ripe figs for 5 minutes in boiling water. Drain. Crush and chop figs. Measure. Boil 5 minutes with just enough water to prevent sticking. Add ¾ cup sugar and 1 tbsp. lemon juice to each cup of figs. Boil until thick. Pour into hot sterilized jars and seal at once.

PICKNEY'S MUD PIE

1¼ cups crushed chocolate wafers
½ gallon coffee ice cream
2 cups whipped cream

½ stick butter, melted
1½ cups fudge sauce
½ cup slivered almonds

Mix crushed wafers and butter. Press into a 9 inch pie plate. (You can use a commercial pie crust). Fill wafer crust with softened ice cream. Freeze until ice cream is firm. Top with cold fudge sauce. Store in freezer for about 10 hours. Top with whipped cream and slivered almonds.

SHEM CREEK SEAFOOD CHOWDER

1 onion, diced
2 carrots, diced
4 stalks celery, diced
2 potatoes, diced large
1 lb. fish of your choice
1 tbsp. garlic, minced
salt & pepper to taste

1 pint heavy cream
1 pint seafood stock
1 lb. shrimp, peeled
1 lb. scallops
1 tsp. dill
5 tbsp. olive oil

In a large skillet sauté onions, carrots, celery, potatoes, dill & garlic in olive oil over medium heat until onions become transparent and begin to simmer. Add heavy cream and seafood stock. Let simmer approximately 30 minutes at a soft boil. Soup will reduce slightly, then add the shrimp, scallops and fish, and let simmer for 15 minutes more.

SOUTH CAROLINA JEWELS

½ stick butter   1 onion, chopped
1 large can diced tomatoes   ½ cup tasso, diced
4 cups baby lima beans, fresh or frozen   2 cups chicken stock
2 tsp. fresh thyme or 1 tsp. dried   salt & pepper to taste

Melt butter in heavy skillet. Bring up temperature and sauté onions until translucent. Add tasso and sauté for 2 minutes. Add remaining ingredients and simmer for 20-30 minutes or until done. Serve over grits.

SWEET POTATO BISCUITS

3 medium sized sweet potatoes, baked or boiled
1 tbsp. sugar   1 egg
2 tbsp. shortening   1 tsp. baking powder
1 cup flour

Mash potatoes. Add shortening and egg, then other ingredients. Do not use any liquid. Add just enough of the flour to make a stiff dough. Roll out, cut and bake at 400° on a lightly greased pan.

THE BEST EGG CUSTARD PIE

3 eggs
½ cup sugar
dash nutmeg

2 cups milk
dash salt

Beat all ingredients together and pour into an unbaked pie crust. Bake at 400° for 35 minutes.